Unsolved!

THE MYSTERY OF ATLANTIS

Kathryn Walker

based on original text by Brian Innes

Crabtree Publishing Company

www.crabtreebooks.com

Crabtree Publishing Company

www.crabtreebooks.com

Author: Kathryn Walker
 based on original text by Brian Innes
Project editor: Kathryn Walker
Picture researcher: Colleen Ruck
Managing editor: Miranda Smith
Art director: Jeni Child
Designer: Rob Norridge
Design manager: David Poole
Editorial director: Lindsey Lowe
Children's publisher: Anne O'Daly
Editor: Molly Aloian
Proofreader: Crystal Sikkens
Crabtree editorial director: Kathy Middleton
Production coordinator: Katherine Berti
Prepress technician: Katherine Berti

Cover: The Atlantis resort in the
Bahamas features a recreation of
the legendary island of Atlantis.

Photographs:
Corbis: Phillippe Giraud/Sygma: front cover; Marco Simoni/
 Robert Harding World Imagery: p. 22–23; Paul Souders: p. 4–5
Fortean Picture Library: p. 15
Istockphoto: Filip Makowski: p. 25; Karen Massier: p. 19;
 Vasiliki: p. 30
Mary Evans Picture Library: p. 6, 8–9, 12–13
NASA: p. 7
Shutterstock: Fast Snail: p. 22–23 (foreground); Karel Gallas: p. 27;
 Agostinho Goncalves: p. 16–17; Lucian: p. 21; Paul Prescott:
 p. 11; Stephen Aaron Rees: p. 20; Rui Vale de Sousa: p. 10
Topfoto: Fotoware Fotostation: p. 28–29; R. Lamb: p. 24, 26;
 Charles Walker: p. 14

Illustration:
Stefan Chabluk: p. 18

Every effort has been made to trace the
owners of copyrighted material.

Library and Archives Canada Cataloguing in Publication

Walker, Kathryn, 1957-
 The mystery of Atlantis / Kathryn Walker ; based on original text by
Brian Innes.

(Unsolved!)
Includes index.
ISBN 978-0-7787-4152-7 (bound).--ISBN 978-0-7787-4165-7 (pbk.)

 1. Atlantis (Legendary place)--Juvenile literature. I.°Innes, Brian. Where
was Atlantis? II. Title. III. Series: Unsolved! (St. Catharines, Ont.)

GN751.W34 2009   j001.94   C2009-903112-4

Library of Congress Cataloging-in-Publication Data

Walker, Kathryn.
 The mystery of Atlantis / Kathryn Walker, based on original text by Brian
Innes.
 p. cm. -- (Unsolved!)
 Includes index.
 ISBN 978-0-7787-4165-7 (pbk. : alk. paper) -- ISBN 978-0-7787-4152-7
(reinforced library binding : alk. paper)
 1. Atlantis (Legendary place)--Juvenile literature. I. Innes, Brian. II. Title.
III. Series.

 GN751.W34 2009
 398'.42--dc22

                                                    2009020925

Crabtree Publishing Company
www.crabtreebooks.com   1-800-387-7650

Published in Canada
Crabtree Publishing
616 Welland Ave.
St. Catharines, ON
L2M 5V6

Published in the United States
Crabtree Publishing
PMB16A
350 Fifth Ave., Suite 3308
New York, NY 10118

Published by CRABTREE PUBLISHING COMPANY in 2010

Contents

A Lost Land 4

The Great Flood 8

The Legend Grows 12

Looking for Atlantis 16

Lost and Found 22

Did Atlantis Exist? 28

Glossary 31

Index 32

Further Reading 32

A Lost Land

...There is a tale of a great island lost beneath the sea.

More than 2,370 years ago, the Greek writer Plato wrote about a huge island in the Atlantic Ocean. He said the island was called Atlantis. The story Plato told about Atlantis has fascinated people for centuries.

Plato said that Atlantis was a rich and very beautiful land. Atlantean people were **advanced** in knowledge and **skills**. However, disaster struck very suddenly and their land was destroyed by earthquakes and floods. Plato said: "In a single dreadful day and night...the island of Atlantis was swallowed up by the sea and vanished."

To this day, no one is sure if Atlantis really existed. People still look for clues to where this great island might have been. Some dream of finding its ruins beneath the sea.

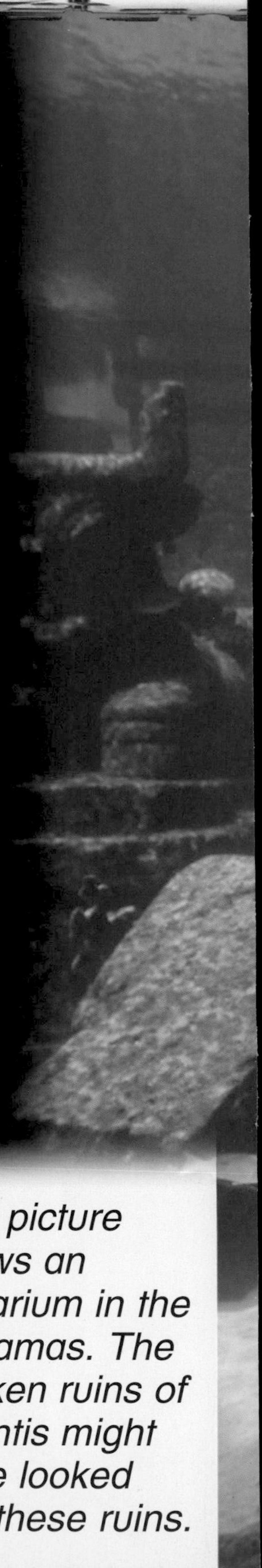

This picture shows an aquarium in the Bahamas. The sunken ruins of Atlantis might have looked like these ruins.

>> **advanced**—Highly developed and ahead of others

"'...the island of Atlantis was swallowed up by the sea...'"

How Strange...

Plato said that the rulers of Atlantis became greedy for power. The gods punished them by destroying Atlantis.

According to Plato, both Atlantis and the Atlantic Ocean were named for Atlas, son of the sea god.

Life in Atlantis

Plato said that Atlantis was the richest land ever known. All kinds of plants and foods grew there. Many types of animals lived on the island, including elephants. The earth was full of precious metals.

The capital city of Atlantis was built on a mountain. The city was surrounded by three rings of water, one inside the other. To protect the city, huge stone walls were built on the land between the rings of water. Each wall was covered in a different metal.

The royal palace and a great temple stood at the center of the city. The temple was covered in silver and gold. It contained an enormous gold statue of **Poseidon**.

The Atlanteans were a powerful people with a huge army and navy. They captured lands as far east as Egypt and as far north as Tuscany in Italy.

"The capital city of Atlantis...was surrounded by three rings of water, one inside the other."

The drawing below shows the city of Atlantis as Plato described it. Bridges cross the rings of water that surround the city.

6

>> **Poseidon**—The Greek god of the sea and bringer of earthquakes

Time and place

Plato said that the story of Atlantis had been told by Egyptian **priests**. He said that Atlantis was destroyed more than 9,000 years before his own time. That is at least 11,500 years ago.

The Greeks of Plato's time were sailors, but they only sailed in the Mediterranean Sea. At the west end of the Mediterranean, a narrow passage of water separates the countries of Morocco and Spain. Today, this passage is known as the Strait of Gibraltar. The Ancient Greeks called it the Pillars of Hercules.

The Greeks knew that the huge Atlantic Ocean was beyond this passage. Plato said this was where Atlantis was, in front of the Pillars of Hercules.

This photograph, taken from space, shows the Strait of Gibraltar. It is the narrow passage of water between the Mediterranean Sea (right) and the Atlantic Ocean (left).

The Great Flood

...Could stories of Atlantis and the Great Flood be linked?

Many people think that what Plato wrote about the land of Atlantis was just **fiction**. But throughout the world, there are legends of the Great Flood. In many legends, the Flood was sent by a god or gods to punish humans for their wickedness. Some people think that the island of Atlantis was destroyed by the Great Flood.

When sailors from Europe first began exploring the Atlantic Ocean, they found islands, such as the Azores, the Canaries, and Madeira. The sailors thought these islands might be the mountain peaks of the sunken land of Atlantis.

Explorers who sailed farther west discovered a huge **continent**. They wondered if this was what remained of Atlantis. Some mapmakers from the 1500s called this land Atlantis, even though it had already been named America.

How Strange...

When the first Spanish explorers went to Mexico, the Aztec people were living there. According to legend, the Aztecs had come from the island of Aztlán. The Spanish thought Aztlán was Atlantis.

>> **fiction**—A story that has been made up and is not based on fact

"...throughout the world, there are legends of the Great Flood."

In this painting, victims of the Great Flood are shown trying to find safe ground. Christians believe, a man named Noah was warned of the Flood and built a boat. His boat is shown in the top right of the painting.

A man of ideas

Ignatius Donnelly was born in Philadelphia in 1831. In 1882, his book titled *Atlantis* was **published**. It was a great success. In this book, Donnelly said he believed Plato's story was true. Atlantis had been a huge landmass situated between Europe and the Americas.

Donnelly said that, when Atlantis was destroyed, some of its people escaped on ships and rafts. They took stories of the disaster to countries east and west of the Atlantic Ocean. These stories survived into modern times and were told around the world.

In his book, Donnelly said Plato placed Atlantis on the Azores islands. In this area, the ocean is not very deep. It is called the mid-Atlantic Ridge. Maybe this area was part of the sunken island of Atlantis.

The Azores islands are shown in this photograph. Donnelly thought they were what was left of the mountains of Atlantis.

"In his book, Donnelly said Plato placed Atlantis on the Azores islands."

>> **published**—Printed and made ready for sale

Proving it

Donnelly claimed that countries on both sides of the Atlantic Ocean shared similar stories and customs. He said this proved that Atlantis once existed in the Atlantic Ocean—it had been the center from which these ideas had spread.

This pyramid is at Chichén Itzá, Mexico. It has steps leading to the temple at the top.

Most of Donnelly's ideas could not be proved. Many of the connections between countries across the Atlantic Ocean were later found to be false or **exaggerated**. For example, Donnelly claimed that in Egypt and Mexico, people had built similar pyramids. But these pyramids are only roughly similar in shape. Those in Mexico had steps leading to a temple at the top. Egyptian pyramids were smooth-sided and built as burial places.

Donnelly's facts may be wrong, but this has not stopped people from reading his book. People continue to write more amazing tales of Atlantis.

How Strange...

 Donnelly thought the gods of ancient Egypt, Greece, India, Scandinavia, and Peru were ancient kings and queens of Atlantis.

The Legend Grows

...Some people have formed new ideas about Atlantis.

During the 1800s, the legend of Atlantis got mixed with tales of other lost lands. One of these was the story of a continent in either the Indian or Pacific Ocean. It was called Lemuria.

In 1904, author W. Scott-Elliot wrote a book about Lemuria. He said Lemuria existed at the time of the **dinosaurs**. According to Scott-Elliot, the Lemurians were more than 10 feet (3 meters) tall and had three eyes. **Aliens** from the planet Venus came to Earth to teach them skills and science. Scott-Elliot said that part of Lemuria began to sink about 100 million years ago. The northern part survived as Atlantis.

This idea of Atlantis was nothing like Plato's ideas. Stories about Atlantis seemed to get more weird and less believable. Then one of these stories turned out to be partly true.

How Strange...

Scott-Elliot said that Lemurians had two eyes that were very far apart and a third eye at the back of their heads.

>> **dinosaur**—A type of reptile, often very large, that lived millions of years ago

"...Lemurians were more than 10 feet (3 meters) tall and had three eyes."

This picture shows what Lemuria may have looked like. Scott-Elliot believed that Lemurians had contact with aliens.

>> **alien**—A creature from another planet, also called an extraterrestrial

Edgar Cayce

Edgar Cayce lived from 1877 to 1945. He seemed to have unusual powers. Cayce would go into a trance, or sleeplike state. Then he would answer questions about the past, present, and future. He said he was in touch with the spirits of dead people.

Cayce answered many questions about Atlantis. He said that Atlanteans had used special crystals to draw energy from the Sun, stars, and Moon. As they became greedy, they used the crystals to get too much power. Unused energy from the crystals ran into the ground and destroyed Atlantis.

Cayce made a **prediction** about Atlantis. He said: "A portion of the temples may yet be discovered under the slime of ages and sea water near Bimini. Expect it in 1968 or 1969—not so far away."

Many people believed that Edgar Cayce, pictured here, had powers that science could not explain.

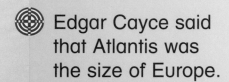

How Strange...

- Edgar Cayce said that Atlantis was the size of Europe.

- Cayce also said that the sinking of Atlantis caused the Great Flood.

>> **prediction**—A warning or statement of what will happen in the future

The Bimini Road

As Cayce predicted, something amazing happened in 1968. Dr. J. Manson Valentine visited the Bahamas. This is a chain of small islands off the coast of Florida. Just off the small island of North Bimini, Dr. Valentine saw a line of huge stones. It looked like a highway under the sea.

In 1975, a team of experts set out to investigate what Dr. Valentine had seen. They found that the stones ran in a straight line for about 1 mile (1.6 kilometers). Then, the stones curved and ran for another 800 yards (730 m). This structure was named "The Bimini Road." It was made from huge stone blocks each about 17 x 17 feet (5 x 5 m).

The sea around the Bahamas began to rise in about 10,000 B.C. In 6000 B.C., the Bimini Road would have been 30 feet (9 m) above **sea level**. Perhaps this ancient roadway was part of Atlantis.

This picture shows some of the stones found in the sea near North Bimini. Some of the stones are rounded, while others, such as the ones shown here, look as if they have been cut.

>> **sea level**—The average level of the sea's surface

Looking for Atlantis

...Where exactly could Atlantis have been?

According to Plato, Atlantis was in the Atlantic Ocean, in front of the Pillars of Hercules. But could he have been wrong? Perhaps the story had changed over the centuries or got mixed up with other tales.

Herodotus was a Greek **historian** who wrote before Plato's time. He traveled widely in lands around the Mediterranean Sea. Herodotus wrote about things he saw and heard. He said there was a mountain far to the west called Atlas. **Natives** living there were called Atlantes.

There is, indeed, a long range of mountains in North Africa called the Atlas Mountains. It is possible that Plato got the name Atlantis from reading Herodotus. Is it also possible that Atlantis was really in North Africa?

The Atlas Mountains loom over a village in Morocco. The mountains also run through the North African countries of Tunisia and Algeria.

>> **historian**—Someone who studies, or is an expert in, history

Greek legends say that a giant named Atlas carried the weight of the sky on his shoulders. He did this on Mount Atlas, the highest peak of the Atlas Mountains.

North Africa

In the 1st century A.D., the Roman historian Pliny wrote that there was an island **opposite** Mount Atlas. He said it was called Atlantis. However, Pliny also wrote that people called Atlantes lived in the middle of the North African desert.

This information, together with what Herodotus said, has made some people believe that Atlantis was not an island continent. Instead, they think it could have been a powerful empire in North Africa. An empire is a collection of lands controlled by one ruler.

"...some people believe that Atlantis was not an island continent."

This map shows some of the places where people think Atlantis may have existed.

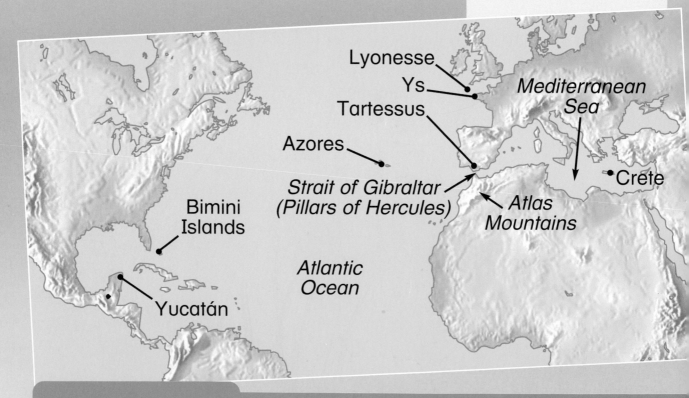

Lyonesse

Ys

Tartessus

Mediterranean Sea

Azores

Strait of Gibraltar (Pillars of Hercules)

Bimini Islands

Atlas Mountains

Crete

Atlantic Ocean

Yucatán

>> **opposite**—Across from and usually facing something

Southern Spain

Tartessus was a wealthy region and city known to the Ancient Greeks. It was a center of **trade**. The exact location of the city is not known. However, descriptions of Tartessus suggest it was near the mouth of the Guadalquivir River on the southern coast of Spain.

If this is true, Tartessus fits Plato's description of Atlantis in several ways. It would have been located in front of the Pillars of Hercules. There would have also been a large plain behind it, backed by mountains, as Plato described. Photos of the area taken from the air show some unusual circular and rectangular forms. The circles match the rings of earth and water that surrounded the city of Atlantis. The rectangles could be the city's temples.

It is likely that Tartessus disappeared when the Guadalquivir River brought down huge amounts of mud from the mountains. The city would have sunk beneath the mud. Could this be what really happened to Atlantis?

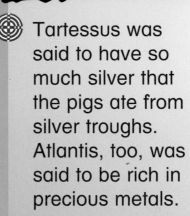

How Strange...

Tartessus was said to have so much silver that the pigs ate from silver troughs. Atlantis, too, was said to be rich in precious metals.

These wetlands are part of the Doñana National Park in Spain. It is possible that Tartessus was located here.

>> **trade**—The purchase, sale, or exchange of goods

More tales

Was Atlantis farther away from the Pillars of Hercules? Northwest France has a legend of the city of Ys that was swallowed by the sea. In England, there are stories about the land of Lyonesse that sank off the southwestern coast. It is said that Lyonesse once joined the Scilly Isles to the coast of England.

St. Agnes is one of the Scilly Isles off the English coast. Legends say these islands were the hilltops of the lost land of Lyonesse.

Geologists are scientists who study Earth's crust—its outer layer of rock—and how it forms. They agree that the countries of Ireland, Britain, and France were once joined together. At that time, the sea was lower than it is today. Much of the world's water was frozen.

As the ice melted, the sea level rose. The **English Channel** filled with water. The water flowed northward to create the North Sea. This happened between 7,400 and 9,000 years ago. Maybe Atlantis was somewhere in this region.

>> **English Channel**—The narrow area of sea separating England and France

A clash of worlds

Immanuel Velikovsky was a Russian-born author. In 1950, he published a book titled *Worlds in Collision*. Velikovsky claimed that about 16,000 years ago, a huge **comet** passed close to Earth. He said that it caused the destruction of Atlantis and other changes throughout the world. Then the comet moved away and became the planet Venus.

Experts say there is nothing to prove Velikovsky's claim. But they agree that huge meteorites have struck Earth. Meteorites are pieces of rock from space that burn up as they get close to Earth. They have caused major changes in the world.

One of the biggest of these meteorites struck Yucatán in Mexico. It has often been suggested that this area was part of the empire of Atlantis. But this event happened millions of years before humans existed.

"...[experts] agree that huge meteorites have struck Earth."

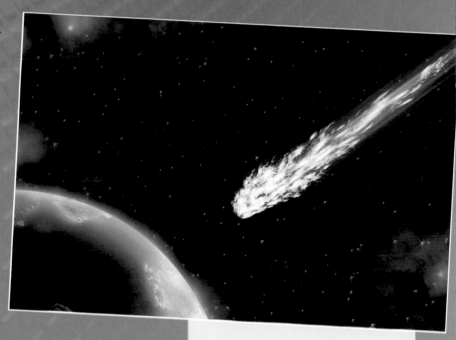

This picture shows an artist's idea of a meteorite heading toward Earth. Could a meteorite such as this have caused the destruction of Atlantis?

Lost and Found

...Some people believe Atlantis has been found in the Mediterranean Sea.

Plato said that Atlantis was destroyed more than 9,000 years before his time. The story he told came from Egypt and had been passed on by **word of mouth**. It is possible that the date Plato gave was wrong. It is also possible that he guessed that Atlantis lay beyond the Pillars of Hercules. Maybe Atlantis was somewhere closer to home.

Before Plato, there is no mention of Atlantis in Greek writings. However, there is mention of a mysterious land called Skeria. This appears in the *Odyssey*, a book by the Greek writer Homer. He wrote it in about 600 B.C.

Homer's description of Skeria sounds very similar to Atlantis. Like Atlantis, Skeria had a palace with golden doors and bronze walls. The mountains around it had many **springs** and rivers. The ground was full of precious metals. But where was Skeria?

>> **word of mouth**—Passed on through speech instead of through writing

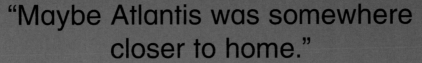

"Maybe Atlantis was somewhere closer to home."

These are ruins of the palace of Knossos on the island of Crete. The pot on the left was found among the ruins. It is possible that Crete was the true location of Homer's Skeria and Plato's Atlantis.

The palace of Knossos

Some experts began to think that Skeria was the Greek island of Crete. Sir Arthur Evans was an English archeologist. An archeologist studies the art and dwellings of people in the past. In the early 1900s, Evans made an amazing discovery while digging in Crete.

Evans found a magnificent palace at Knossos. There were paintings on its walls that showed men and women leaping over a charging bull. Interestingly, Plato said that people fought with bulls inside the main temple of Atlantis.

It was clear that this **civilization** of Crete was very important. It is now called the Minoan civilization and it began in about 3000 B.C. Could Crete have been part of Atlantis?

How Strange...

 Greek legends told the story of King Minos who lived at Knossos. The Minoan civilization was named for him.

This wall painting is from the Palace of Knossos. It shows young people leaping over a bull.

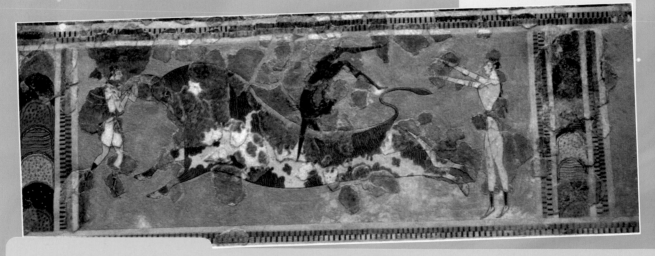

>> **civilization**—A very organized society that has developed in a particular region

Thera connection

Spiros Marinatos was a Greek archeologist. In the 1930s, Marinatos found volcanic ash on the north coast of Crete. He wondered if the Minoan civilization had been destroyed by a volcanic **eruption**. When volcanos erupt, thousands of tons of ash can be hurled into the air. Eruptions under the sea can also cause huge tidal waves. This sounds like what happened to Atlantis.

Less than 100 miles (160 km) north of Crete is the volcanic island of Thera, also known as Santorini. In about 1500 B.C., Thera erupted. The center of the island was blown away. Winds carried the ash hundreds of miles away.

In 1967, Marinatos went to Thera to find out if people lived there before the eruption. Beneath the ash, he found the remains of an ancient sea port. The art and pottery he found there were like those found on Crete. Thera seemed to have been part of the Minoan civilization.

This is the island of Thera. In about 1500 B.C., it was the site of one of the largest volcanic eruptions the world has known.

When a volcano explodes, thousands of tons of ash may be **hurled** into the air, as this picture shows.

Water and ash

From what Marinatos found on Thera and Crete, he was able to form a picture of what had happened there thousands of years before. First, there would have been earthquakes underground. Then the volcano exploded.

The movement of land beneath the sea caused a tidal wave. This struck the north coast of Crete less than one hour after the eruption. Then ash from the volcano fell on Knossos. The ash would have filled the sky, blocking out the Sun. The ash made the water undrinkable. Nothing could grow. Minoan life on Thera and at Knossos ended.

"The ash would have filled the sky, blocking out the Sun."

>> **hurled**—Thrown or flung with great force

A question of time

The destruction of Thera and Knossos seems likely to have been the true story of Atlantis. The two stories match in many ways, but the dates are very different. Thera erupted in about 1500 B.C. Plato says that Atlantis disappeared thousands of years before that date.

According to Plato, the story came from Egypt. Mistakes may have been made when it was **translated** from Egyptian to Greek. People have suggested that the Egyptian symbol for one hundred was mistaken for one thousand. This mistake would bring Plato's date for the end of Atlantis closer to the date of Thera's eruption.

How Strange...

 The Palace of Knossos was made up of more than 1,000 rooms. It covers an area of about 24,000 square yards (20,000 square meters).

A painting of dolphins decorates this room in the Palace of Knossos. Part of the palace has been rebuilt to look as it once did.

>> **translated**—Changed from one language into another

Did Atlantis Exist?

...People still argue over whether Atlantis was fact or fiction.

The idea of Atlantis has captured people's imaginations for centuries. It has been used in novels, games, and comic books. Television series and movies have also been based on the story.

But was Atlantis ever more than just an idea? It is possible that Plato never meant for his story to be read as a true history. He tells us about a civilization that seemed almost perfect. But then he says it was destroyed by the gods because of its people's greed. In just one day and night, Atlantis was wiped out.

Maybe the story of Atlantis was meant as a warning to the people of Ancient Greece. It warns that even great civilizations can turn bad. The story is also a reminder of how the most powerful **nations** can be destroyed by the forces of nature.

>> **nation**—A country and the people who live in it

How Strange...

- The television series *Stargate Atlantis* locates Atlantis in another galaxy.

- Jules Verne's novel *Twenty Thousand Leagues Under the Sea*, features a visit to Atlantis in a submarine.

The legend of Atlantis has been the subject of many movies. This picture is from the movie Atlantis: The Lost Empire.

Like many folk tales or legends, the Atlantis story could be a mixture of fact and fiction. Plato could have based it on one or more stories that he had heard. Some people believe that what Plato described was a single, real event.

Likely sources

If this is true, then it seems likely he was describing the destruction at Thera and Knossos. The volcanic eruption was one of the biggest in human history. It was a story that would have been retold over the centuries. The details could have been exaggerated and changed.

New discoveries also suggest that Tartessus in Spain could have been Atlantis. In 2005, a **fragment** of pottery was found in southern Spain. It had an unusual pattern of circles, one inside the other. Some people think this represents the rings of land and earth around the city of Atlantis.

However, it is unlikely that the story will end in either Knossos or Spain. There is something about the story of a lost land under the sea that excites and fascinates people. The search for Atlantis continues.

"...the Atlantis story could be a mixture of fact and fiction."

This picture shows a statue of the great writer and thinker, Plato, who lived between 428 and 347 B.C.

>> **fragment**—A small piece that has been broken off

Glossary

advanced Highly developed and ahead of others

alien A creature from another planet, also called an extraterrestrial

civilization A very organized society that has developed in a particular region

comet A mass of dust and gas that moves around the Sun

continent A large landmass, such as North America, Africa, or Asia

dinosaur A type of reptile, often very large, that lived millions of years ago

English Channel The narrow area of sea separating England and France

eruption The sudden release of lava and ash when a volcano explodes or erupts

exaggerated Said to be bigger or greater than in real life

fiction A story that has been made up and is not based on fact

fragment A small piece that has been broken off

historian Someone who studies, or is an expert in, history

hurled Thrown or flung with great force

nation A country and the people who live in it

native A person born and living in a particular place

opposite Across from and usually facing something

Poseidon The Greek god of the sea and bringer of earthquakes

prediction A warning or statement of what will happen in the future

priest Someone who performs religious ceremonies

published Printed and made ready for sale

sea level The average level of the sea's surface

skill The ability to do something well, usually through training or practice

spring A place where water rises up out of the ground

subject Something or someone talked or written about

trade The purchase, sale, or exchange of goods

translated Changed from one language into another

word of mouth Passed on through speech instead of through writing

31

Index

aliens 12, 13
Atlantic Ocean 4, 5, 7, 8, 10, 11, 16, 18
Atlantis,
  city of 6, 19, 22, 24, 30
  destruction of 4, 5, 8, 10, 14, 21, 25, 27, 28
  location of 4, 7, 8, 10, 14, 15, 16–21, 22, 23, 24, 27, 30
  people of 4, 5, 6, 10, 11, 14, 28
Atlas Mountains 16–18
Azores 8, 10, 18
Aztlán 8

Bimini 14, 15, 18

Cayce, Edgar 14, 15
comets and meteorites 21
Crete 18, 23, 24, 25, 26

Donnelly, Ignatius 10–11

earthquakes 4, 26
Egypt 6, 7, 11, 22, 27
Evans, Sir Arthur 24

floods 4, 8, 9, 14

gods 5, 6, 8, 11, 28

Herodotus 16, 18
Homer 22, 23

Knossos 23, 24, 26, 27, 30

Lemuria 12–13
Lyonesse 18, 20

Marinatos, Spiros 25, 26
Mediterranean Sea 7, 16, 18, 22
Mexico 8, 11
  Yucatán 18, 21
Minoan civilization 24–26

North Africa 16–18

Pillars of Hercules
  see Strait of Gibraltar
Plato 4, 5, 6, 7, 8, 10, 12, 16, 19, 22, 24, 27, 28, 30
Pliny 18
pyramids 11

Scilly Isles 20
Scott-Elliot, W. 12–13
Skeria 22, 23, 24
Strait of Gibraltar 7, 16, 18, 19, 20, 22

Tartessus 18, 19, 30
Thera (Santorini) 25, 26, 27, 30
tidal waves 25, 26

Valentine Dr. J. Manson 15
Velikovsky, Immanuel 21
volcanic eruption 25, 26, 27, 30

Ys 18, 20

Further Reading

• Deary, Terry. **Greek Legends**, "Twisted Tales" series. Scholastic, 2004.
• Martin, Michael. **Atlantis**, "Edge Books" series. Capstone Press, 2007.
• Scarre, Chris & Stefoff, Rebecca. **The Palace of Minos at Knossos**, "Digging for the Past" series. Oxford University Press, USA, 2003.
• Wallace, Holly. **The Mystery of Atlantis**, "Can Science Solve?" series. Heinemann, 2006.